D0248476

THE CITY OF BATH

Photographs by Bob Croxford

The Georgian City of Bath is one of the most beautiful cities in the world.
From earliest times the hot springs have given the city its synonymous name.
The Romans came and left behind the Great Baths and much else. In
Georgian times Bath became the height of fashionable entertaining and a
stylish place to live. The architecture from this time is justly famous.

Many of the pictures in this, and other Atmosphere books, are available as large photo prints to fra
For details of sizes and prices please see www.atmosphere.co.uk/prints.html

Published by Atmosphere
Willis Vean
Mullion Cornwall TR12 7DF
England
Tel 01326 240180
email info@atmosphere.co.uk

All images Copyright Bob Croxford 200
All Moral Rights Reserved

ISBN 0 9543409 8 1

Printed and bound in Italy

All images Copyright Bob Croxford 200
All Moral Rights Reserved

Cover: The Royal Crescent

Frontispiece: THE GORGON'S HEAD found at the site of the Roman

Water fountain

Hot water from the Overflow from the King's Bath

THE ROMAN BATH at night with the Abbey beyond

The atmospheric GREAT BATH filled with hot spa water

THE FOUNTAIN at the edge of the Roman Bath

The dramatic setting of the ROMAN BATHS at night

Ancient stone plinths border the ROMAN BATH

The ROMAN BATH is in the heart of the City of Bath and is overlooked by the Abbey

One of several statues look down on the ROMAN BATH

Roman Legionnaires once bathed in the ROMAN BATH

Tranquil reflections

Pathways of stone are well worn

PIGEONS now play and bathe where Romans once did.

Looking down on THE KING'S BATH

THE ABBEY at night

THE ABBEY reflected in the River Avon   THE ABBEY and THE PUMP ROOM at night

THE ABBEY stands proudly above the City

THE ABBEY'S west front reflected in a shop window

An angel climbs a ladder on the front face of THE ABBEY THE ABBEY from Beechen Cliff

ABBEY GREEN is tucked away to the south of the Abbey

PULTENEY BRIDGE at night reflected in the River Avon

A Pleasure boat passes under PULTENEY BRIDGE

The refreshing sound of splashing water can always be heard at THE HORSESHOE WEIR

Early morning on PULTENEY BRIDGE looking east

A flower shop on PULTENEY BRIDGE

Shops line both sides of PULTENEY BRIDGE

PULTENEY BRIDGE reflected in the River Avon

The bedding displays in PARADE GARDENS are amongst the finest in the country   Relaxation in PARADE GARDENS   33

Summer flowers in PARADE GARDENS

THE ROYAL CRESCENT from ROYAL VICTORIA PARK

The Lawn in front of THE ROYAL CRESCENT

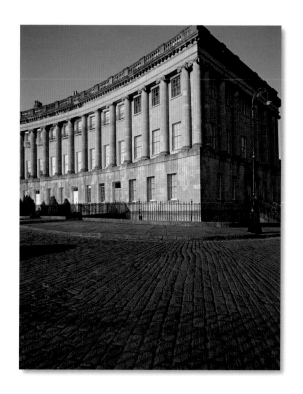

ONE, THE ROYAL CRESCENT is preserved as a museum of Georgian living

Dusk in THE ROYAL CRESCENT

The Georgian sweep of THE ROYAL CRESCENT

The Palladian Bridge at Prior Park is a masterpiece of Georgian garden design

Iron railings line THE ROYAL CRESCENT

The fountain at LAURA PLACE marks the start of Great Pulteney Street   LANSDOWN CRESCENT looks down over Bath

White doors and weathered limestone in BRUNSWICK PLACE

BRUNSWICK PLACE detail

45

Terraced houses follow the contours in RIVER STREET

BELVEDERE on Lansdown Road climbs out of the City

BELMONT's builders coped with the steep hillside with elegance

The golden stonework of SYDNEY PLACE

Bath's famed Georgian architecture in THE CIRCUS

THE CIRCUS, John Wood the elder's masterpiece

Smart and elegant window boxes abound in BATH

Bath's NEW THEATRE ROYAL is one of the oldest theatres in the country

Bust of actor and playwright DAVID GARRICK (1717-1779)

This stone lion guards the entrance to VICTORIA GARDENS

Narrowboats moor on the Kennet and Avon Canal at BATHAMPTON   The K&A CANAL passes under a house near Sydney Gardens

SALLY LUNN'S HOUSE is reputedly the oldest house in Bath. It was here she made the famous Sally Lunn buns

A trompe l'oeil painting on a window filled in to avoid the 1696 -1851 window tax

Ivy-clad traditional Georgian house

INDEX

Abbey Green	24
Bathampton	58
Belmont	48
Belvedere	47
Brunswick Place	44, 45
Coat of Arms	56
David Garrick	55
Georgian Buildings	62
Gorgon's Head	1
Great Pulteney St	42
Horseshoe Weir	27
Kennet and Avon Canal	58, 59
King's Bath	16
Lansdown Crescent	43
Laura Place	42
New Theatre Royal	54, 55
Overflow	4
Parade Gardens	32, 33, 34
*Prior Park	40
Pulteney Bridge	25, 26, 28 - 31
Pump Rooms	19
River St	46
Road Sign	64
Roman Baths	5 - 15
Royal Victoria Park	35, 37, 57
Sally Lunn's House	60
Sydney Place	49
The Abbey	17 - 23
The Circus	50, 51
The Royal Crescent	Cover, 35, 36-39, 41
Water Fountain	3
Window boxes	52, 53
Window tax	61

*With kind permission of the National Trust

leaf: Road sign on the way to Bath